To: _____

From: _____

Date: _____

Happily Ever After

This book is dedicated to Ryan — the one who knows the good, the bad, and everything in between about me, and loves me more because of it.

—Brittany

© 2024 Brittany Anne Mormann
All rights reserved.

No part of this book may be reproduced in any form whatsoever, whether by graphic, visual, electronic, film, microfilm, tape recording, or any other means, without prior written permission of the publisher, except in the case of brief passages embodied in critical reviews and articles.

The opinions and views expressed herein belong solely to the author and do not necessarily represent the opinions or views of Cedar Fort, Inc. Permission for the use of sources, graphics, and photos is also solely the responsibility of the author.

ISBN 13: 978-1-4621-4772-4
ebook ISBN 13: 978-1-4621-4773-1

Published by Plain Sight Publishing, an imprint of Cedar Fort, Inc.
2373 W. 700 S., Suite 100, Springville, UT 84663
Distributed by Cedar Fort, Inc., www.cedarfort.com

LIBRARY OF CONGRESS CATALOGING-IN-PUBLICATION DATA

Cover design and interior layout and design by Shawnda T. Craig
Cover design © 2024 Cedar Fort, Inc.

Printed in the United States of America

10 9 8 7 6 5 4 3 2 1

Printed on acid-free paper

100 questions FOR COUPLES

CONNECT your THOUGHTS

Brittany Anne Mormann

AND THEY LIVED HAPPILY EVER...

Wait, wait, wait! The story doesn't end there. In fact, it's only just beginning. The wedding bells are finished ringing, the honeymoon is over, and the presents have been opened (and maybe exchanged). Now it's just you and your spouse figuring out how to actually live "happily ever after."

In a world with over 8 billion people, you two managed to meet and fall in love. What are the odds? I actually don't know the odds, but I'm going to go out on a limb and say that it was pretty lucky that you two found each other.

Do you remember when you first met? You probably went through that awkward stage where you asked each other good ol' ice breaker questions like...Where are you from? How old are you? Where do you work? What do you like to do for fun? I am sure you

1

also played the "what's your favorite…" game. What's your favorite color? What's your favorite food? What's your favorite movie?

As you kept dating and got to know each other better, those superficial types of questions slowed down and you started asking deeper questions that would help you to know if this relationship had a future. It's those deeper questions that brought me to the creation of this book.

I have read tons of relationship books, listened to hundreds of relationship experts and podcasts, and watched all the rom-coms and Hallmark movies. They all have one thing in common that is so crucial to relationships: COMMUNICATION. And not just any communication, I'm talking about good, honest, healthy communication about the things that matter most in your marriage.

Having a strong connection with your spouse starts with good communication. I have known couples who tell me that they talk all the time and still have problems, but talking doesn't always mean communicating. Are you just talking or are you truly communicating when you discuss your future together? Are you talking about your hopes and dreams? Are you communicating your fears about things to come? Are you sharing your goals? Are you talking out loud about your expectations?

It's been said that men are not mind readers, but, fun fact, neither are women. The only real way to find out what someone is thinking is to get them to open up by asking good questions.

I saw a sign once that said, "Marriage is like a deck of cards. In the beginning all you need is two hearts and a diamond, but by the end, you wish you had a club and a spade." The whole point of this book is to try and prevent the need for a club and a spade. It is meant to help you start having conversations about things that are important when starting your life together. It is meant to be fun, but at the same time it is meant to provide valuable information for both of you. Your answers are not set in stone. As life changes, so will your thoughts and opinions on things. This will just get the thoughts flowing on different subjects so that you can simultaneously connect with your partner and make sure you're on the same page.

As you go through each of these questions, my only request is that you do 2 things:

1. Be honest with your responses. Honesty is the foundation of all successful marriages.

2. Listen. And I mean really listen. Ask clarifying questions to make sure you are hearing what your significant other is saying.

Can I take this moment to focus on the word "significant" in significant other? The Oxford definition of significant is: "sufficiently great or important to be worthy of attention." Worthy of attention! Give them your attention by truly listening to what they are saying.

Now go Connect Your Thoughts!!

This first set of
questions has to do with
your thoughts about your
wedding and honeymoon

After that, the questions
are pretty random.

1.

How do you feel the overall planning of the wedding went from engagement to wedding?

Would you have done anything differently?

2.

Were you happy with the
wedding festivities?
(reception, luncheon, bridal shower, bachelor party, etc.)

Why or why not?

3.

Did you like where we
chose to get married?

4.

Were you okay with how much money was spent on the

wedding and honeymoon?

What was worth or not worth the money?

5.

Did someone come to the wedding that you did not expect?

Did someone not come that you were really wanting to be there?

6.

What was the BEST PART
of the wedding day?

(Besides marrying your best friend).

7.

What was your favorite gift?

What was your least favorite gift?

8.

Did something happen at the wedding that was *unexpected?*

9.

If you could change ONE THING about the wedding day, what would it have been?

10.

What is something that went great during the honeymoon? (besides the obvious ;)

Did something happen during the *honeymoon* that you didn't expect?

12.

Would you pick that
honeymoon spot again?

Keep talking about your wedding day! Come up with a fun annual tradition to do on your anniversaries like watching your wedding video or looking through your wedding photo album, dancing to your wedding song, or eating the same kind of cake you had.

Now onto the random questions...

13.

How often should we have
DATE NIGHTS
now that we're married?

14.

How often should we have

DATE NIGHTS

once we have kids?

15.

Do you think it is okay to hang out with **FRIENDS** without the other being there?

If so, how often should we hang out separately with our friends?

16.

Video games are fun, but can take up a lot of time. How much time do you think is acceptable to be playing video games each day/week?

This question can be changed for any leisure activity that takes up a lot of your time (reading, sports, watching TV/movies, DND, etc.).

17.

How much time do you think is acceptable to spend on cellphones?

Whether it's messaging or social media, what limits or settings do we want in place to make sure that we stay present and *connected to each other?*

18.

What are your thoughts on having pets?

Should we get a pet when we have kids?

What kind of pet(s) do you think we should get?

How should we go about dividing up the roles of taking care of pets?

19.

How often should we eat at home?

EAT OUT?

Eat at our families houses?

20.

How should we figure out what's for dinner and who cooks it?

21.

What is your favorite and
least favorite *chore* to do?

(Maybe you can do each other's least favorite chore.)

How should we divide up the inside
and outside chores?

22.

Do you like or want a nickname/pet name for each other?

23.

What is your *cleanliness* standard for each room?

In other words, in order for a room to truly be clean, what does that look like to you?

24.

Should certain chores be done before
we go to bed each night?

Should the dishes be done before
bed each night?

Should the floors be swept? Etc.

25.

What are your top 3 priorities right now?

26.

Are there off limits topics that you would prefer I

DIDN'T TALK ABOUT

with other people?

27.

How often do you want/need to
talk to your parents?

28.

How often do you want/need to
see your parents?

29.

How often should our parents come visit us?

Are you okay with **SURPRISE** visits?

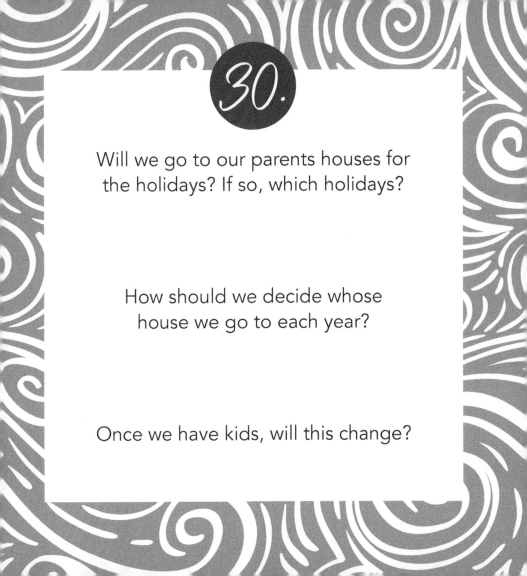

30.

Will we go to our parents houses for the holidays? If so, which holidays?

How should we decide whose house we go to each year?

Once we have kids, will this change?

31.

What family **TRADITIONS** are important to you that you want to continue in our family?

32.

What is your *love* language?

This is so important to know in order to be a good partner. (If you don't know yours already, there are online quizzes and books that can help.)

33.

How do you handle conflicts at *work?*

Do you put off addressing it or do you tackle it head on?

34.

How do you handle conflicts with those in your *family?*

Do you brush it off or confront it?

How do you go about that?

35.

When do you think it is okay to text/call someone from the opposite gender that is not related to you?

When do you think it is inappropriate?

36.

When you are having a bad day,
what can I do to help?

Do you need space?

Do you want to talk about it right away?

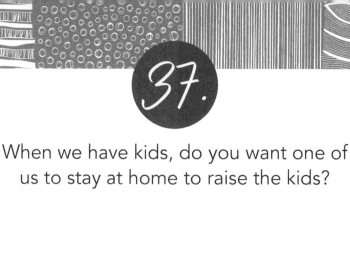

37.

When we have kids, do you want one of us to stay at home to raise the kids?

If both of us are working, who will be watching the kids?

38.

Who do you want to be
IN THE HOSPITAL
room when our kids are born?

39.

When it comes to naming our kids, are there family names that you want to use?

40.

Do you want to find out ahead of time what the gender of our baby is going to be?

Do you want a *gender reveal party?*

41.

What is your go-to activity to relax
or to take your mind off of things?

42.

What is your dream job that you would do even if you never got paid for it?

43.

What do you want our
RETIREMENT to look like?

How old do you want to be
when you/we retire?

44.

Would you consider yourself
a saver or a spender?

45.

What do you feel is **WORTH** going into debt for?

46.

What are things you are okay spending a lot of money on?

(vacations, cars, jewelry, purses, etc.)

47.

When it comes to making big purchases, should we talk about those together or is it okay to make those purchases on our own?

48.

What do you want intimacy in the
bedroom to look like?

Anything you want to try? Not try?

49.

How often would you like to be intimate?

50.

Are you okay if I talk to others about our *intimate life?*

51.

If I don't like something (intimacy wise), how and when would you like me to go about telling you?

52.

If we can't have kids naturally, are you okay with fostering or adopting?

How long should we try to have kids naturally before we consider other options?

53.

Is there anything you want to do
or accomplish before we
start having kids?

54.

What should our birthing plan be?

(natural, epidural, midwife, home birth, hospital, etc.)

55.

What parenting style do you think you most relate to?

(You can find these different parenting styles explained online.)

56.

How was your childhood upbringing?

What did you love about it?

What did you not like about it?

57.

How much *involvement* do you want our parents to have in our marriage?

How much *involvement* do you want our parents to have with raising our kids?

58.

What important events do you want
our parents to be a part of?

59.

Is regularly attending
a church important to you?

60.

Should we raise our children

in a certain *religion?*

61.

What do you like to do in your alone time?

How often do you feel that you
NEED TIME ALONE?

62.

Do you want to vacation with just us, with friends and family, or a little bit of both?

63.

Should we have our own HOBBIES that we don't do together?

64.

Is exercising important to you?

Should we EXERCISE together?
If so, what should we do?

65.

What values do you want to
instill in our *kids?*

66.

Is there a *dream vacation* place that you want to go visit?

67.

What is your favorite quality
about me?

68.

What is the most important thing you think all relationships should have?

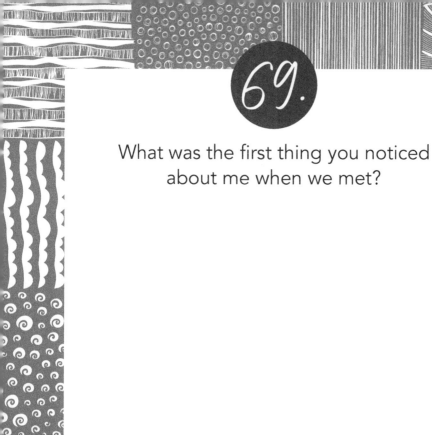

69.

What was the first thing you noticed about me when we met?

70.

Which of your family members
are you most like?

WHY?

71.

What does the

perfect date night

look like to you?

72.

What worries do you have about

HAVING KIDS?

73.

Do you consider yourself a
competitive person?

Do you feel it is okay to be
competitive in a relationship?

74.

What is a quality in your parents' relationship that you want in our relationship?

What is a quality that you do not want?

75.

What is on your bucket list?

76.

What do you think are our
STRENGTHS as a couple?

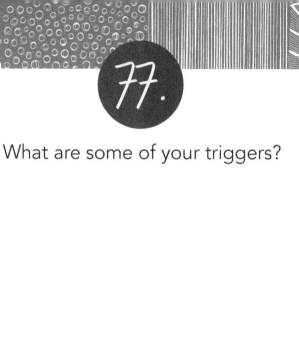

77.

What are some of your triggers?

78.

What is something you want to *improve* about yourself?

79.

What is your most recent big

accomplishment?

80.

What gives you
ENERGY?

81.

What drains you of energy?

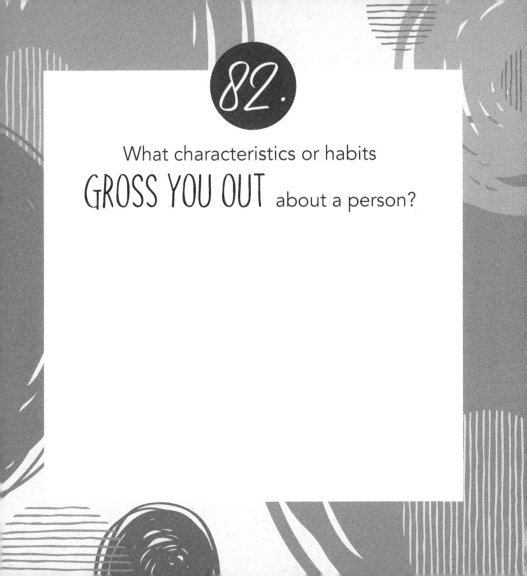

82.

What characteristics or habits
GROSS YOU OUT about a person?

83.

What makes you feel safe and secure?

84.

How do you feel about
public displays of affection?

85.

If one of us has a serious addiction, how should we go about getting through it?

If we see it in a close friend or family member, how should we help them?

86.

Do you think there are *secrets* that are okay to keep from one another?

If so, what kind of secrets?

87.

What do you think is the ideal
work schedule before we have kids?

After we have kids?

88.

When you are feeling stressed,
how do you handle it?

89.

What are situations that a relationship
can not come back from?

90.

How do you want to celebrate
each other's *birthdays?*

I plan it, you plan it, we plan it, no plans?

91.

How should we manage our finances?

92.

What activity makes you really happy when you are doing it (not counting intimacy)?

93.

Do you like to be *surprised?*

94.

How would you describe yourself
when you are sick?

Do you like to be taken care of?

HOW?

95.

If you are working on a project or task, do you want to work on it together or do you prefer to work alone?

96.

Should we combine our finances
or keep them separate?

97.

Would you consider yourself someone
who is quick or slow to apologize?

What does a meaningful apology
look like to you?

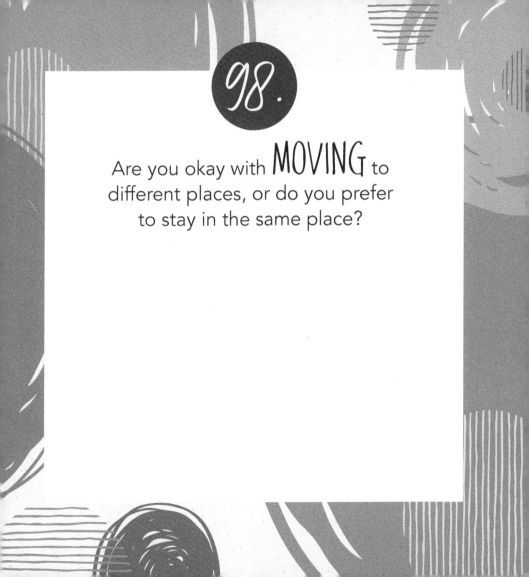

98.

Are you okay with **MOVING** to different places, or do you prefer to stay in the same place?

99.

If I had to tell you *bad news*, would you rather me be direct with you, or would you prefer that I *break it to you gently?*

100.

Use all the letters of our last name to describe *qualities* that you want in our *marriage*.

I promise to *always*...